DE
IN
OF
OUR MOTHER OF
PERPETUAL HELP

Official Edition

Liguori
ONE LIGUORI DRIVE
LIGUORI MO 63057-9999

Imprimi Potest.
John F. Dowd, C.SS.R.
Provincial, St. Louis Province
The Redemptorists

Imprimatur:
+ John N. Wurm, Ph.D., S.T.D.
Vicar General, Archdiocese of St. Louis

© 2000, Liguori Publications
ISBN-13: 978-0-7648-0411-3
Printed in the United States of America
07 08 8 7

Liguori Publications, a nonprofit corporation, is an apostolate of the Redemptorists. To learn more about the Redemptorists, visit Redemptorists.com.

To order, call 1-800-325-9521
www.liguori.org

Cover design by Christine Kraus

(1) Greek initials for 'Mother of God."
(2) Greek initials for "St. Michael the Arch-angel." He is depicted holding the lance and spear with the vessel of vinegar and gall of Christ's Passion.
(3) Greek initials for "St. Gabriel the Arch-angel." He holds the Cross and the nails.
(4) Greek initials for "Jesus Christ."

When the miraculous picture of Our Mother of Perpetual Help was enshrined in the church of St. Alphonsus in Rome, in 1866, Pope Pius IX commanded the Redemptorists: "Make Our Mother of Perpetual Help known throughout the world."

For over a hundred years Redemptorists have continued to spread devotion to the Mother of God. Literally millions of people have been motivated by their sermons on Mary. Through their efforts, millions of pictures of Our Mother of Perpetual Help have been distributed throughout the world.

May this booklet of novena prayers help to deepen and strengthen your devotion to Mary, the Mother of the Church, and Our Mother of Perpetual Help. Through that devotion may you, too, make her known to others.

Table of Contents

Hymns

O Mother
of Perpetual Help

1) O Mother of Perpetual Help,
   To thee we come imploring help.
Behold us here, from far and near,
   To ask of thee our help to be;
Behold us here, from far and near,
   To ask of thee our help to be.

2) Perpetual help we beg of thee;
   Our souls from sin and sorrow free;
Direct our wandering feet aright,
   And be thyself our own true light;
Direct our wandering feet aright,
   And be thyself our own true light.

3) And when this life is o'er for me,
   This last request I ask of thee:
Obtain for me in heaven this grace,

To see my God there face to face:
Obtain for me in heaven this grace
To see my God there face to face.

Immaculate Mary

1) Immaculate Mary, your praises we sing
   Who reigns now with Christ, our
       Redeemer and King.
   Ave, Ave, Ave, Maria! Ave, Ave, Maria!

2) In heaven the blessed your glory proclaim
   On earth we, your children, invoke
       your fair name.
   Ave, Ave, Ave, Maria! Ave, Ave, Maria!

Perpetual Help Hymn

1) Come let us follow
   Where God himself led.
   Unto the image of her
   Who has said:
   I am your own Perpetual Help.

2) Come, sick and troubled
   With stories untold,
   This is your mother,
   Look up and behold,
   She is your own Perpetual Help.

O Mary My Mother

1) O Mary my Mother,
   to thee do I flee
   In all my afflictions
   I hasten to thee
   Thy heart is so gentle,
   so loving, so mild
   Thou canst not reject
   a poor suppliant child.

2) O Mary my Mother,
   I'm longing to see
   The glory thy Son
   has bestowed upon thee
   That heaven of glory
   so purely thine own
   Reward which thy virtues,
   thy purity won.

Hail, Holy Queen
Enthroned Above

1) Hail, holy Queen enthroned above,
   O Maria.
   Hail, Queen of mercy and of love,
   O Maria.
   Triumph, all ye Cherubim,
   Sing with us, ye Seraphim,
   Heaven and earth resound the hymn:
   Salve, Salve, Salve Regina.

2) The cause of joy to men below,
   O Maria.
   The spring through which all graces
   flow,
   O Maria.
   Angels, all your praises bring,
   Earth and heaven, with us sing,
   All creation echoing:
   Salve, Salve, Salve Regina.

Mother Dear,
Oh, Pray for Me

1) Mother dear, oh, pray for me,
    Whilst, far from heaven and thee,
I wander, in a fragile bark,
    O'er life's tempestuous sea.
O Virgin Mother, from thy throne
    So bright in bliss above,
Protect thy child, and cheer my path
    With thy sweet smile of love.

Chorus

Mother dear, oh, pray for me,
    And never cease thy care.
'Til in heaven eternally,
    Thy love and bliss I share.

2) Mother dear, oh, pray for me
    Should pleasure's siren lay
E'er tempt thy child to wander far
    From virtue's path away.
When thorns beset life's devious way
And darkling waters flow,

Then, Mary, aid thy weeping child,
　　Thyself, a mother show.

Chorus

Mother Dearest, Mother Fairest

1) Mother dearest, Mother fairest,
　　Help of all who call on thee,
Virgin purest, brightest, rarest,
　　Help us, help, we cry to thee.

Chorus

Mary help us, help, we pray;
　　Mary help us, help, we pray;
Help us in all care and sorrow,
　　Mary help us, help, we pray

2) Lady, help in pain and sorrow,
　　Soothe those racked on bed of pain.
May the golden light of morrow
　　Bring them health and joy again.

Chorus

Remember Holy Mary

1) Remember, holy Mary,
    'Twas never heard or known
That anyone who sought thee
    And made to thee his moan,
That anyone who hastened
    For shelter to thy care,
Was ever yet abandoned
    And left to his despair.

2) And so to thee, my Mother,
    With filial faith I call,
For Jesus dying gave thee
    As Mother to us all.
To thee, O Queen of virgins,
    O Mother meek, to thee
I run with trustful fondness,
    Like child to mother's knee.

Daily, Daily Sing to Mary

1) Daily, daily sing to Mary,
      Sing, my soul, her praises due:
All her feasts, her actions honor
      With the heart's devotion true.
Lost in wondering contemplation,
      Be her majesty confessed:
Call her Mother, call her Virgin,
      Happy Mother, Virgin blest.

2) She is mighty in her pleading,
      Tender in her loving care;
Ever watchful, understanding,
      All our sorrows she will share.
Advocate and loving Mother.
      Mediatrix of all grace:
Heaven's blessings she dispenses
      On our sinful human race.

Public Prayers in Honor of

OUR MOTHER OF PERPETUAL HELP

(Biblical/Liturgical)

Opening Hymn (Stand)

PRIEST: Most holy and Immaculate Virgin and our Mother Mary, you are our Perpetual Help, our refuge and our hope.

ALL: We come to you today. * We thank God for all the graces received through your intercession. * Mother of Perpetual Help, we promise to love you always * and to do all we can to lead others to you.

PRIEST: Mother of Perpetual Help, confident of your powerful influence with God, obtain for us these graces:

ALL: The strength to overcome temptation, * a perfect love for Jesus Christ, * and a holy death * so that we will live with you and your Son for all eternity.

****

PRIEST: Let us pray to be open to God's Word.

ALL: Mother of Perpetual Help, * you continually sought the meaning of God's words and actions in your life. * As we listen to God's Word, * may the Holy Spirit enlighten our understanding * and give us the courage * to put his Word into practice in our daily lives.

(If homily follows, all should be seated.)

****

PRIEST: Let us kneel to pray as a community of faith. Mary, all generations have called you blessed, and the Almighty has done great things for you.

ALL: Mother of Perpetual Help, * we call upon your most powerful name. * Your very name inspires confidence and hope. * May it always be on our lips, * especially in times of temptation * and at the hour of our death. * Blessed Lady, help us whenever we call on you. * Let us not be content with merely pronouncing your name. * May our daily lives proclaim * that you are our Mother and our Perpetual Help.

※ ※ ※ ※ ※ ※

PRIEST: Let us pray for our temporal wants.

ALL: Mother of Perpetual Help, * with the greatest confidence we kneel before you. * We implore your help in the problems of our daily lives. * Trials and sorrows often depress us; * misfortunes and privations bring misery into our lives; * everywhere we meet the cross. * Comforter of the Afflicted, * beg your Son Jesus * to strengthen us as we bear our burdens * and to free us from our sufferings. *

Or if it be the will of God * that we should suffer still longer, * help us endure all with love and patience. * May we follow the example of your Son, * and through him, * with him, * and in him * commend ourselves to the care of our heavenly Father.

******

PRIEST: Let us stand now to present our petitions and our thanks. Lord Jesus Christ, at a word from Mary your Mother, you changed water into wine at Cana of Galilee. Listen now to the People of God gathered here to honor Our Mother of Perpetual Help. Grant our petitions and accept our sincere thanks.

Grant wisdom and guidance to our Holy Father, Pope..., our Bishop..., our priests, and all the leaders of our nation, state, and community.

ALL: Hear us, Lord, through Mary our Mother.

PRIEST: Grant peace and unity throughout the world, especially in our homes and families.

ALL: Hear us, Lord, through Mary our Mother.

PRIEST: Grant that young people respond generously to the call of the Holy Spirit in deepening their faith and choosing their vocation in life.

ALL: Hear us, Lord, through Mary our Mother.

PRIEST: Grant us continued health of mind and body, and help the sick, especially..., to regain their health according to your holy will.

ALL: Hear us, Lord, through Mary our Mother.

PRIEST: Grant eternal rest to all our deceased, especially..., and to the souls of all the faithful departed.

ALL: Hear us, Lord, through Mary our Mother.

PRIEST: Let us pause now to silently present our own petitions to Our Mother of Perpetual Help.

Lord, accept our thanks for the new life of grace you gave us.

ALL: We thank you, Lord, through Mary our Mother.

PRIEST: Accept our thanks for all the graces received through the sacramental life of the Church.

ALL: We thank you, Lord, through Mary our Mother.

PRIEST: Accept our thanks for the spiritual and material blessings we have received.

ALL: We thank you, Lord, through Mary our Mother.

PRIEST: Let us pause now to silently thank Our Mother of Perpetual Help for our own favors received.

******

PRIEST: Please kneel as we pray for the sick.

ALL: Lord, look upon your servants * laboring under bodily weakness. * Cherish and revive the souls * which you have created * so that, purified by their sufferings, * they may soon find themselves healed by your mercy. * We ask this through Christ our Lord. Amen.

PRIEST: May the Lord Jesus Christ be with you that he may defend you, within you that he may sustain you, before you that he may lead you, behind you that he may protect you, above you that he may bless you in the name of the Father, the Son, and the Holy Spirit.

ALL: Amen.

******

PRIEST: Let us renew our confidence in Mary as a perpetual help.

ALL: Mother of Perpetual Help, * you have been blessed and favored by God. * You became not only the Mother of the Redeemer * but the Mother of the redeemed as well. * We come to you today as your loving children. * Watch over us and take care of us. * As you held the child Jesus in your loving arms, * so take us in your arms. * Be a mother ready at every moment to help us. * For God who is mighty * has done great things for you, * and his mercy is from age to age * on those who love him. * Our greatest fear is * that in time of temptation, * we may fail to call out to you, * and become lost children. * Intercede for us, dear Mother, * in obtaining pardon for our sins, * love for Jesus, * final perseverance, * and the grace always to call upon you, * Mother of Perpetual Help.

✳✳✳✳✳✳

*(The following Act of Consecration
is to be said the first week of the month.)*

PRIEST: Let us renew our Act of Consecration.

ALL: United with the members of your confraternity * here and throughout the world, * we consecrate ourselves to your service. * We promise to renew this dedication once a month * and frequently to receive the sacraments. * We beg you to obtain for us * the grace to imitate your great servant, St. Alphonsus, * in his love for you and your Son.

✳ ✳ ✳ ✳ ✳ ✳

PRIEST: Let us stand now and unite with the Christians of all ages in praising Mary and in committing ourselves to her powerful protection.

ALL: Hail Mary, etc.

PRIEST: Pray for us, O holy Mother of God.

ALL: That we may become worthy of the promises of Christ.

PRIEST: Let us pray. Lord Jesus Christ, who gave us your Mother Mary, whose image we venerate, as a mother ready at every moment to help us; grant, we beg you, that we who call on her help may always enjoy the fruit of your redemption. This we ask through you who live and reign forever.

ALL: Amen.

Public Prayers in Honor of

OUR MOTHER OF PERPETUAL HELP

(Mary Our Model)

Opening Hymn (Stand)

PRIEST: Let us kneel as we gather together to honor our Mother and our Perpetual Help. We recall how she helped others. Her whole life was a lesson in love.

ALL: Mother of Perpetual Help, * today we face so many difficulties. * Your picture tells us so much about you. * It reminds us to reach out and help those in need. * Help us understand * that our lives belong to others * as much as they belong to us. * Mary, model of Christian love, * we know we cannot heal every ill * or solve every problem. * But with

God's grace, * we intend to do what we can. * May we be true witnesses to the world * that love for one another really matters. * May our daily actions proclaim * how fully our lives are modeled after yours, * Mother of Perpetual Help.

******

PRIEST: Mary, you were a woman of steadfast faith. Your faith in Jesus never wavered. Model of all believers, pray to the Holy Spirit for us. Help us not only to accept all your Son teaches us but to put that teaching into practice.

ALL: Mother of Perpetual Help, * as a child, * Jesus ran to you for comfort and reassurance. * You did not see him as only a frail child. * Moved by the Holy Spirit, * you accepted Jesus as the Son of the Most High, * the long-awaited Messiah. * Following your example of faith, * help us recognize Jesus in those we meet, * especially the poor and the lonely, * the sick and the elderly. * Keep us always mindful, dear Mother, * that whatever we do to the least of our brothers and sisters, * we do to your loving Son. * May his words live in our hearts * and influence our lives * and the lives of those we meet.

******

PRIEST: Let us pray to be open to God's Word.

ALL: Mary, woman of faith, * you pondered and treasured the meaning of God's words and actions in your life. * You generously responded to his Word in faith. * As we listen to God's Word * help us be attentive to his message. * May the Holy Spirit enlighten our understanding, * and give us the courage to put these words into practice.

(If homily follows, all should be seated.)

******

PRIEST: Let us stand as we present our petitions. Grant wisdom and guidance to our Holy Father, Pope..., our Bishop..., our priests, and all the leaders of our nation, state, and community.

ALL: May your Mother intercede for us, Lord.

PRIEST: Grant peace and unity throughout the world, especially in our homes and families.

ALL: May your Mother intercede for us, Lord.

PRIEST: Grant that young people respond generously to the call of the Holy Spirit in deepening their faith and choosing their vocation in life.

ALL: May your Mother intercede for us, Lord.

PRIEST: Grant us continued health of mind and body, and help the sick, especially..., to regain their health according to your holy will.

ALL: May your Mother intercede for us, Lord.

PRIEST: Grant eternal rest to all our deceased, especially..., and to the souls of all the faithful departed.

ALL: May your Mother intercede for us, Lord.

PRIEST: Let us pause now to silently present our own personal petitions to Our Mother of Perpetual Help.

******

PRIEST: Let us kneel as we continue our prayers:

ALL: Mary, humble handmaid of the Lord, * we need your example today * to discover God's will in our lives. * You always gave God the first place in your life. * Just as you pondered his Word in your heart, * help each of us to seek his plan in all that we do. * Give us the conviction * that nothing is more important * than doing the will of our heavenly Father. * May we spend each moment in loving and pleasing him. * Help us follow your example in proclaiming, * I am the servant of the Lord. * I will what God wills, * when he wills it, * as he wills it, * because he wills it.

* * * * * *

PRIEST: Mother of Perpetual Help, your picture reminds us that we are to carry our cross as Jesus did. With courage, he endured injustice, abandonment and betrayal, pain and suffering, even a criminal's death.

ALL: Mary, we turn to you as our model in suffering and courage. * You shared in your Son's suffering and death. * Now you share in his Resurrection. * We, too, share in the Cross of Christ, * and someday, like you, * we will share fully in his Resurrection. * Help us be patient in our suffering, * and to trust in the loving care of our Father in heaven. * May those suffering sickness in mind or body * experience your Son's healing power. * Help us follow his example, * and through him, *

with him, * and in him, * commend ourselves
to the care of our heavenly Father.

✱ ✱ ✱ ✱ ✱ ✱

PRIEST: Let us ask Mary to watch over all
families.

ALL: Mother of Perpetual Help, * bless our
families with your tender, motherly love. *
May the sacrament of marriage * bring hus-
bands and wives ever closer together * that
they may always be faithful, * and love each
other as Christ loves us. * Help all mothers
and fathers love and cherish the children *
God has entrusted to them. * May they
always be models of a truly Christian life. *
Help all children, * that they may love and
respect their parents. * Inspire all people * to
value Christian marriage and family life. *
Give us a sense of responsibility * that we
may do our part * in making our homes
havens of love and peace. * Mary, our model,
* help every family grow daily * in genuine

31

love for God and neighbor * so that justice and peace may flourish everywhere in the human family.

✳ ✳ ✳ ✳ ✳ ✳

(The following Act of Consecration is to be said the first week of the month.)

PRIEST: Let us renew our Act of Consecration.

ALL: United with the members * of the Confraternity of Our Mother of Perpetual Help * here and throughout the world, * we consecrate ourselves to your service. * We promise to renew this dedication once a month * and frequently to receive the sacraments. * We beg you to obtain for us * the grace to imitate your great servant, St. Alphonsus, * in his love for you and your Son.

✳ ✳ ✳ ✳ ✳ ✳

PRIEST: From the first moment of her existence, the Holy Spirit filled Mary with his love. By his power, she became the Virgin-Mother of God. Through the same Holy Spirit, she became the perfect wife, the perfect mother. Let us imitate her generosity, her openness to the Holy Spirit, and say,

ALL: Come, Holy Spirit. * Fill our hearts with your joy and your peace, * with your power and your love, * with your constant Presence within us.

PRIEST: Receive the Holy Spirit. May he be with you to strengthen you, above you to protect you, before you to lead you, behind you to encourage you, within you to possess you totally. Through the prayers of our holy patron, St. Alphonsus, through the intercession of Our Mother of Perpetual Help, through the merits of our Lord and Savior Jesus Christ, present in the Most Blessed Sacrament of the altar, may the blessing of

almighty God, the Father, Son, and Holy
Spirit, descend upon you and remain forever.

ALL: Amen.

Public Prayers in Honor of

OUR MOTHER OF PERPETUAL HELP

(Eastern Edition)

Opening Hymn (Stand)

Reading of Petitions and Thanksgivings

(All kneel to recite the prayers together, pausing at the asterisk *.)

Behold at thy feet, O Mother of Perpetual Help, * a wretched sinner who has recourse to thee and confides in thee. * O Mother of Mercy, have pity on me. * I hear thee called by all * the refuge and the hope of sinners; * be then, my refuge and my hope. * Assist me for the love of Jesus Christ; * stretch forth thy hand to a miserable, fallen creature * who recommends himself to thee, * and who devotes himself to thy service forever. * I bless and thank almighty God, * who in his mercy has given me this confidence in thee, * which I hold to be a pledge of my eternal salvation. * It is true, dearest Mother, * that in the past I have miserably fallen into sin * because I had not recourse to thee. * I know, however, that with thy help I shall conquer; * I know, too, that thou wilt assist me * if only I recommend myself to thee. * But I fear, dear Mother, * that in time of danger * I may neglect to call on thee and thus lose my soul. * This grace, then, I ask of thee, * and this I beg with all the fervor of my soul, * that in all the attacks of hell * I may ever have recourse to thee. * O Mary, help me! * O Mother of Perpetual Help, never suffer me to lose my God.

Three Hail Marys.

O Mother of Perpetual Help, * grant that I may ever invoke thy most powerful name, * which is the safeguard of the living and the salvation of the dying. * O purest Mary, O sweetest Mary, * let thy name henceforth be ever on my lips. * Delay not, O Blessed Lady, * to help me whenever I call on thee, * for, in all my needs, in all my temptations * I shall never cease to call on thee, * ever repeating thy sacred name, Mary, Mary. * O, what consolation, * what sweetness, * what confidence fill my soul, * when I pronounce thy sacred name, * or even only think of thee. * I thank God for having given thee, for my good, * so sweet, so powerful, so lovely a name. * But I will not be content with merely pronouncing thy name; * let my love for thee prompt me ever to hail thee, * Mother of Perpetual Help.

Three Hail Marys.

PRIEST: Let us here pause for a few moments in silent prayer to recommend to our Mother of Perpetual Help all our wants both spiritual and temporal.

O Mother of Perpetual Help, * thou art the dispenser of all the goods * which God grants to us miserable sinners, * and for this reason he has made thee so powerful, so rich, and so bountiful, * that thou mayest help us in our misery. * Thou art the advocate of the most wretched and abandoned sinners * who have recourse to thee. * Come then, to my help, dearest Mother, * for I recommend myself to thee. * In thy hands I place my eternal salvation * and to thee do I entrust my soul. * Count me among thy most devoted servants; * take me under thy protection, and it is enough for me. * For, if thou protect me, dear Mother, * I fear nothing; * not from my sins, * because thou wilt obtain for me the pardon of them; * nor from the devils, * because thou art more powerful than all hell together; * nor even from Jesus, my Judge himself, * because by one prayer from thee * he will be appeased. * But one thing I fear, * that in the hour of temptation * I may neglect to call on thee * and thus perish miserably. * Obtain for me, then, the pardon of my sins, * love for Jesus, * final perseverance, * and the grace always to have recourse to thee, * O Mother of Perpetual Help.

Three Hail Marys.

PRIEST: Thou hast been made for us, O Lady, a refuge.

ALL: A helper in need and tribulation.

PRIEST: Let us pray. O Lord Jesus Christ, who hast given us thy Mother, Mary, whose renowned image we venerate, to be a mother ever ready to help us, grant, we beseech thee, that we who constantly implore her help may merit always to experience the fruits of thy redemption, thou who livest and reignest world without end.

ALL: Amen.

Prayer of St. Alphonsus

Most Holy and Immaculate Virgin and my Mother, Mary, * to thee, who art the Mother of my Lord, the Queen of the world, * the advocate, the hope, and the refuge of sinners, * I have recourse today, * I who am the most miserable of all. * I render thee my most humble homage, O great Queen, * and I thank thee for all the graces * thou hast obtained for me until now, * and in particular for having saved me from hell which I have so often deserved. * I love thee, O most amiable Lady; * and, for the love which I bear thee, * I promise to serve thee always * and to do all in my power to make others also love thee. * I place in thee all my hopes * and I confide my salvation to thy care. * Accept me for thy servant * and receive me under thy mantle, * O Mother of Mercy. * And since thou art so powerful with God, * deliver me from all temptations, * or, rather, obtain for me the strength to triumph over them until death. * Of thee I ask a perfect love for Jesus Christ; *

through thee I hope to die a good death. * O my Mother, * by the love which thou bearest to God, * I beseech thee to help me at all times * but especially at the last moment of my life. * Leave me not, I beseech thee, * until thou seest me safe in heaven, * blessing thee and singing thy mercies for all eternity. * Amen, so I hope; so may it be.

Act of Consecration

(to be said once each month on the day chosen by the Novena Director)

Desiring to consecrate myself entirely * to the service of the ever Blessed Virgin Mary, * from whom, after God, * I expect all help and assistance * in life and in death, * I unite myself with the members * of this pious confraternity, * which has been erected * in honor of Our Mother of Perpetual Help. *

As my special patron * I choose the glorious St. Alphonsus, * that he may obtain for me * a true and lasting devotion * to the ever Blessed Virgin, * who is honored by so sweet a name.

I promise, moreover, * to renew my consecration * to the Mother of God and to St. Alphonsus * once a month * and frequently to receive the holy sacraments.

O Mother of Perpetual Help, * receive me as thy servant, * and grant that I may ever experience * thy constant motherly protection. * I promise to have recourse to thee * in all my spiritual and temporal necessities. * My holy patron, St. Alphonsus, * obtain for me * the grace of an ardent love for Jesus Christ, * and the grace of ever invoking * the Mother of Perpetual Help.

Public Prayers in Honor of

OUR MOTHER OF PERPETUAL HELP

(Western Edition)

Opening Hymn (Stand)

Reading of Petitions and Thanksgivings

(All kneel to recite the prayers together, pausing at the asterisk*.)

Prayer in Spiritual Wants

O Mother of Perpetual Help, * with the greatest confidence, we come before thy sacred picture, * in order to invoke thine aid. * Thou hast seen the wounds which Jesus has been pleased to receive for our sake; * thou hast seen the Blood of thy Son flowing for our salvation; * thou knowest how thy Son desires to apply to us the fruits of his redemption. * Behold, we cast ourselves at thy feet, * and pray thee to obtain for our souls the graces we stand so much in need of. * O Mary, most loving of all mothers, * obtain for us from the heart of Jesus, the source of every good, * these graces * *(here mention them)*. O Mother of Perpetual Help, * thou desirest our salvation far more than we ourselves: * thy Son has given thee to us for our Mother; * thou hast thyself chosen to be called Mother of Perpetual Help. * We trust not in our merits, but in thy powerful intercession; * we trust in thy goodness; * we trust in thy motherly love. * Mother of Perpetual Help, * for the love thou bearest to Jesus, thy Son and our Redeemer, * for the love of thy great servant Alphonsus, * for the love of our souls, * obtain for us the graces we ask from thee. * Amen.

Three Hail Marys.

Prayer in Temporal Wants

O Mother of Perpetual Help, * numerous clients continually surround thy holy picture, * all imploring thy mercy. * All bless thee as the assured help of the miserable; * all feel the benefit of thy motherly protection. * With confidence, then, do we present ourselves before thee in our misery. * See, dear Mother, the many evils to which we are exposed; * see how numerous are our wants. * Trials and sorrows often depress us; * reverses of fortune and privations, often grievous, bring misery into our lives; * everywhere we meet the cross. * Have pity, compassionate Mother, on us and on our dear ones, * especially in this our necessity * *(here mention it)*. Help us, dear Mother, in our distress; * deliver us from all our ills; * or, if it be the will of God that we should suffer still longer, * grant that we may endure all with love and patience. * These

graces we expect of thee with confidence, *
because thou art our Perpetual Help. * Amen.

Three Hail Marys.

For Graces of Salvation

O Mother of Perpetual Help, * thou art
the dispenser of all the goods * which God
grants to us miserable sinners, * and for this
reason, he has made thee so powerful, so rich,
and so bountiful, * that thou mayest help us
in our misery. * Thou art the advocate of the
most wretched and abandoned sinners * who
have recourse to thee. * Come, then, to my
aid, dearest Mother, * for I recommend
myself to thee. * In thy hands I place my eternal salvation * and to thee do I entrust my
soul. * Count me among thy most devoted
servants; * take me under thy protection, and
it is enough for me. * For, if thou protect me,
dear Mother, * I fear nothing; * not from my
sins, * because thou wilt obtain for me the
pardon of them; * nor from the devils, *

because thou art more powerful than all hell together; * nor even from Jesus, my Judge himself, * because, by one prayer from thee, * he will be appeased. * But one thing I fear; * that, in the hour of temptation, * I may neglect to call on thee, * and thus perish miserably. * Obtain for me, then, the pardon of my sins, * love for Jesus, * final perseverance, * and the grace always to have recourse to thee, * O Mother of Perpetual Help.

Three Hail Marys.

PRIEST: Thou hast been made for us, O Lady, a refuge.

ALL: A helper in need and tribulation.

PRIEST: Let us pray. O Lord Jesus Christ, who hast given us thy Mother Mary, whose renowned image we venerate, to be a Mother ever ready to help us; grant, we beseech thee, that we who constantly implore her help may merit always to experience the fruits of thy redemption, thou who livest and reignest world without end.

ALL: Amen.

Prayer of St. Alphonsus

Most Holy and Immaculate Virgin and my Mother, Mary, * to thee, who art the Mother of my Lord, the Queen of the world, * the advocate, the hope, and the refuge of sinners, * I have recourse today, * I who am the most miserable of all. * I render thee my most humble homage, O great Queen, * and I thank thee for all the graces * thou hast obtained for me until now, * and in particular for having saved me from hell which I have so often deserved. * I love thee, O most amiable Lady; * and, for the love which I bear thee, * I promise to serve thee always * and to do all in my power to make others also love thee. * I place in thee all my hopes * and I confide my salvation to thy care. * Accept me for thy servant * and receive me under thy mantle, * O

Mother of Mercy. * And since thou art so powerful with God, * deliver me from all temptations, * or, rather, obtain for me the strength to triumph over them until death. * Of thee I ask a perfect love for Jesus Christ; * through thee I hope to die a good death. * O my Mother, * by the love which thou bearest to God, * I beseech thee to help me at all times * but especially at the last moment of my life. * Leave me not, I beseech thee, * until thou seest me safe in heaven, * blessing thee and singing thy mercies for all eternity. * Amen, so I hope; so may it be.

Act of Consecration

(to be said once each month on the day chosen by the Novena Director)

Desiring to consecrate myself entirely * to the service of the ever Blessed Virgin Mary, * from whom, after God, * I expect all help and assistance * in life and in death, * I unite myself with the members * of this pious confraternity, * which has been erected * in honor of Our Mother of Perpetual Help. *

As my special patron * I choose the glorious St. Alphonsus, * that he may obtain for me * a true and lasting devotion * to the ever Blessed Virgin, * who is honored by so sweet a name.

I promise, moreover, * to renew my consecration * to the Mother of God and to St. Alphonsus * once a month * and frequently to receive the holy sacraments.

O Mother of Perpetual Help, * receive me as thy servant, * and grant that I may ever experience * thy constant motherly protection. * I promise to have recourse to thee * in all my spiritual and temporal necessities. * My holy patron, St. Alphonsus, * obtain for me * the grace of an ardent love for Jesus Christ, * and the grace of ever invoking * the Mother of Perpetual Help.

Litany of Our Lady

Lord, have mercy on us.
Christ, have mercy on us.
Lord, have mercy on us.
Christ hear us.
Christ, graciously hear us.
God, the Father of heaven,
Have mercy on us.
God, the Son, Redeemer of the world,
Have mercy on us.
God, the Holy Spirit,
Have mercy on us.
Holy Trinity, one God,
Have mercy on us.
Holy Mary,
Pray for us.
Holy Mother of God,
Holy Virgin of virgins,
Mother of Christ,
Mother of divine grace,

Mother most pure,
Mother most chaste,
Mother inviolate,
Mother undefiled,
Mother most amiable,
Mother most admirable,
Mother of good counsel,
Mother of our Creator,
Mother of our Savior,
Virgin most prudent,
Virgin most venerable,
Virgin most renowned,
Virgin most powerful,
Virgin most merciful,
Virgin most faithful,
Mirror of justice,
Seat of wisdom,
Cause of our joy,
Spiritual vessel,
Vessel of honor,
Singular vessel of devotion,
Mystical rose,
Tower of David,
Tower of ivory,

House of gold,
Ark of the covenant,
Gate of heaven,
Morning star,
Health of the sick,
Refuge of sinners,
Comforter of the afflicted,
Help of Christians,
Queen of angels,
Queen of patriarchs,
Queen of prophets,
Queen of apostles,
Queen of martyrs,
Queen of confessors,
Queen of virgins,
Queen of all saints,
Queen conceived without original sin,
Queen assumed into heaven,
Queen of the most holy Rosary,
Queen of peace,

Lamb of God, who take away the
  sins of the world,
    Spare us, O Lord.
Lamb of God, who take away the
  sins of the world,
    Graciously hear us, O Lord.
Lamb of God, who take away the
  sins of the world,
    Have mercy on us.

PRIEST: Pray for us, O holy Mother of God.

ALL: That we may be made worthy of the promises of Christ.

PRIEST: Let us pray. Pour forth, we beseech you, O Lord, your grace into our hearts; that as we have known the incarnation of Christ your Son by the message of an angel, so, by his Passion and Cross, we may be brought to the glory of the Resurrection; through the same Christ, our Lord.

ALL: Amen.

Private Prayers

For Conversion of Sinners

Mother of Perpetual Help, you know so well the value of an immortal soul. For every soul has been redeemed by the precious blood of your divine Son. Hear my prayer as I plead for the conversion of a sinner, one who is quickly heading for eternal ruin. I know that you are the refuge of sinners. I know also that God has given you the power to bring about the conversion of even the most hardened sinner. Until now, nothing has been successful in changing this person's sinful way of life. Obtain from your Son the grace of conversion. Merciful Mother, you have brought about the conversion of many sinners through the prayers of their relatives and friends. Listen to my prayer and bring about a true conversion for this unhappy soul. Mother of

Perpetual Help, show that you really are the Refuge of Sinners.

In Sickness

Mother of Perpetual Help, you know how much I suffer because of my sickness. Not only my body but my soul is also affected. I do not even have the strength to pray as I should. Nothing gives me any relief. Even the visits and compassion of my friends bring me no comfort. My courage is beginning to fail; impatience and sadness are having their effect on me. Most tender and loving Mother, in my feelings of distress, I put all my trust in you. Your compassionate heart will surely have pity on me. Merciful Mother, do not forget your devoted, afflicted child's *(here mention your sickness)*. Ask your Son, Jesus, to give me the courage and strength to accept my sickness as the will of God and to bear it with patience and resignation. If it is God's will, intercede for me in recovering my former good health; but if it is God's will that I continue to suffer, or, that this sickness should lead me to a better life, I am perfectly resigned. Loving Mother, I am confident you will obtain the grace to do whatever God asks of me. Amen.

For Financial Aid

Mary, our Mother, we know that you are our Perpetual Help, not only in our spiritual need but in our material need as well. With humble hearts and childlike confidence we beg you to help us in our present financial stress. Due to unforeseen circumstances, we are now in dire need, since we cannot meet our just debts. Dear Mother, we are not asking for wealth or prosperity, but merely for help in satisfying our pressing obligations. You are the Queen of heaven and earth, and, as such, the dispenser of so many favors granted by your Son, Jesus. We know you are most kind and generous to all your devoted children. Loving Mother, we plead with you to obtain the financial help we so desperately need in our present situation. We thank you, dear Mother, and promise to make your perpetual help known far and wide. Amen.

To Know One's Vocation

Mother of Perpetual Help, behold at your feet a humble and loving child. I need your help to recognize and follow the vocation in life that God has planned for me. Mother of Perpetual Help, I know I can more easily be saved in that state of life to which I have been called through the graces of your divine Son. My only desire is to follow God's will in everything that concerns my future. For then I know I shall succeed in working out my eternal salvation. Guide and direct me in choosing the vocation in which I may best fulfill God's divine plan here on earth, and be assured of seeing and possessing him for all eternity. Amen.

How to Make a Novena

No fixed rules need be laid down, generally speaking, for the making of a novena beyond that of persevering in prayer through the space of nine days. The efficacy of the novena prayers depends in great measure on the piety and devotion of the individual.

The *Solemn Novena* in honor of our Mother of Perpetual Help consists of nine successive days of public prayer at a novena church or shrine, usually before some great feast of our Lady, such as the feast of the Immaculate Conception. The *Perpetual Novena* is so called because the public novena services are held on a specified day each week, such as Tuesday, and continue all through the year. Thus a novena of Tuesdays can be begun or concluded at any time during the year. A *Private Novena* can be undertaken by a family or an individual at any time.

The following suggestions will increase the fervor of your novena prayers:

1. Participate, if possible, in the public novena services, since there is added efficacy in the union of the faithful at prayer.

2. Receive the sacraments of Reconciliation and Holy Communion during your novena.

3. Promise our Lady an act of public gratitude, should your petition be granted; have holy Mass celebrated in thanksgiving; make your favor public for the encouragement of others; spread devotion to Mary.

4. Invite others to join in the novena services.

How to Join the Archconfraternity

The Archconfraternity is a worldwide spiritual organization whose members are united for the express purpose of honoring and serving the Mother of God under the special title of "Our Mother of Perpetual Help." It is canonically established at the church of St. Alphonsus in Rome, where the original miraculous image of Our Mother of Perpetual Help is venerated.

To become a member of the Archconfraternity, it is necessary 1) to be enrolled by name at a church or shrine where a confraternity is canonically erected (any Catholic in good standing is eligible); and 2) to recite the Act of Consecration, page 41 or page 49.

Members are urged (not obligated):

1. to renew this Act of Consecration once a month;
2. to have recourse to our Mother of Perpetual Help in every need;
3. to have a Perpetual Help picture in their homes;
4. to wear a medal of Our Mother of Perpetual Help;
5. to spread this devotion among others.

Members of the Archconfraternity enjoy many benefits:

1. They are assured of the constant protection of Our Mother of Perpetual Help.
2. They share in the public devotions and all other good works of the millions of members throughout the world.
3. Through this devotion they are endowed with a remarkable influence for converting obstinate sinners.

4. By the express will of the Superior General of the Redemptorists, they participate in the good works performed by the entire Congregation of Redemptorist Fathers and Brothers throughout the world.

Other Helpful Resources

Marian Prayers and Devotions

Beautiful prayers designed to help Catholics in their devotion to the Mother of the Lord. Includes basic prayers, devotions, prayers for Marian feasts, and other works for both private and public prayer.
Deluxe pamphlet • $1.95

The Story of Our Mother of Perpetual Help

This video explores the legacy of one of the Church's most revered icons—explaining the symbolism, the style, the message, and the story behind the famous picture.
30 minutes • $19.95

Let's Pray (Not Just Say) the Rosary

Meditations for each bead of the rosary.
Deluxe pamphlet • $1.95

How to Get More Out of the Rosary

Rosary meditations to help readers learn to conform to God's will by living a life of faith, hope, and love.
Pamphlet • $1.00

Order from your local bookstore or write to
Liguori Publications
Box 060, Liguori, MO 63057-9999
Please add 15% to your total for shipping and handling ($3.50 minimum, $15 maximum). For faster service, call toll-free 1-800-325-9521, Dept. 060. Please have your credit card handy.